Desert Dwellers

Holly Karapetkova
J. Jean Robertson

Rourke
Publishing LLC
Vero Beach, Florida 32964

www.rourkepublishing.com

PHOTO CREDITS: © Martin Garnham: Cover; © Rusty Dodson: Title Page, 8, 9, 23; © susaro: illustrations; © Mike Norton: page 3, 22; © Maxim Petrichu: page 5; © Steven Love: page 7; © Alexander Hafeman: page 10, 11, 22; © David T. Gomez: page 13, 23; © Lynn Stone: page 15; © Daniel Gilbey: page 17, 23; © Mike Golay: page 19; © VM: page 22 top

Editor: Jeanne Sturm

Cover design by: Nicola Stratford, Blue Door Publishing

Interior design by: Renee Brady

Library of Congress Cataloging-in-Publication Data

Karapetkova, Holly.
  Desert dwellers / Holly Karapetkova and J. Jean Robertson.
    p. cm. -- (My first science library)
  ISBN 978-1-60472-535-3
  1. Desert animals--Juvenile literature. I. Robertson, J. Jean. II. Title.
  QL116.K37 2009b
  591.754--dc22
                        2008025164

Printed in the USA

CG/CG

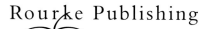

Rourke Publishing

www.rourkepublishing.com – rourke@rourkepublishing.com
Post Office Box 3328, Vero Beach, FL 32964

Many animals you may know live in **deserts**, too. Turn the pages with me now, and we will meet a few.

Turtles live in deserts. Their shells are hard and strong.

4

5

Rabbits live in deserts. Their ears are soft and long.

6

7

Snakes live in deserts. They have dry and scaly skin.

8

9

Camels live in deserts.
Their humps store
fat within.

11

The ostrich lives in deserts. On the ground, it builds a nest.

12

13

Wrens live in deserts. On a **cactus** they may rest.

15

Dorcas **gazelles** live in deserts, but they are very rare.

16

17

Hedgehogs live in deserts. They're covered with spiny hair.

18

19

Deserts are dry and oh, so hot, but I like visiting here a lot!

20

21

Glossary

cactus (KAK-tuhss): A cactus is a plant that grows in dry areas. A cactus has a thick trunk with sharp spikes instead of leaves.

camels (KAM-uhls): Camels may have either one or two humps on their backs. They can travel far without needing water. Camels are used to carry people and goods across deserts.

deserts (DEZ-urts): Deserts are dry, often sandy, areas. Many plants and animals can not live in deserts because there is little rain or water.

Dorcas gazelles (DOR-kuhss guh-ZELS): Dorcas gazelles are a graceful type of antelope. Gazelles are the second fastest running animal. Only cheetahs can run faster.

hedgehogs (HEJ-hogs): Hedgehogs are small, nocturnal animals that eat bugs. They have spiny hair that is stiff with sharp points. To protect himself from enemies, a hedgehog rolls up into a thorny ball.

snakes (SNAYKS): Snakes are animals in the reptile family. They are long and thin. They slither along the ground because they do not have legs. Some snakes are poisonous, and some are not.

Index

Further Reading

Galko, Francine. *Desert Animals*. Heinemann, 2002.

National Geographic Society. *Creatures of the Desert World*. National Geographic Children's Books, 4th Edition, 1991.

Websites

www.arthur.k12.il.us/arthurgs/desanim.htm

www.mbgnet.net/sets/desert/animals/valley.htm

About the Authors

Holly Karapetkova, Ph. D., loves writing poems for kids and adults. She teaches at Marymount University and lives in the Washington, D.C., area with her husband, her son K.J., and her two dogs, Muffy and Attila.

J. Jean Robertson, also known as Bushka to her grandchildren and many other kids, loves to read, travel, and write books for children. After teaching for many years, she retired to San Antonio, Florida, where she lives with her husband.